MISSOURI

HELLO
U.S.A.

by Rita C. LaDoux

Lerner Publications Company

You'll find this picture of a flowering dogwood tree at the beginning of each chapter in this book. The flowering dogwood is the state tree of Missouri. In the spring, these beautiful trees are covered in white or pink blossoms.

Cover (left): The Ozark Plateau covered with morning fog. Cover (right): The Saint Louis skyline, including the Gateway Arch and Mississippi River. Pages 2–3: A section of rapids on the Black River. Page 3: Neon lights and theaters in Branson.

This book is available in two editions:
Library binding by Lerner Publications Company, a division of Lerner Publishing Group
Soft cover by First Avenue Editions, an imprint of Lerner Publishing Group
241 First Avenue North
Minneapolis, MN 55401 U.S.A.

Website address: www.lernerbooks.com

Library of Congress Cataloging-in-Publication Data

LaDoux, Rita, 1951–
     Missouri / by Rita C. LaDoux. (Rev. and expanded 2nd ed.)
        p.   cm. — (Hello U.S.A.)
     Includes index.
     ISBN: 0–8225–4069–X (lib. bdg. : alk. paper)
     ISBN: 0–8225–4140–8 (pbk. : alk. paper)
     1. Missouri—Juvenile literature. [1. Missouri.] I. Title. II. Series.
F466.3 .L33 2002
     977.8—dc21   2001001163

Manufactured in the United States of America
1 2 3 4 5 6 – JR – 07 06 05 04 03 02

CONTENTS

The Missouri River flows across the state and empties into the Mississippi River.

THE LAND

Rivers, Plains, and Plateaus

way, we're bound away, 'cross the wide Missouri," sang wistful travelers as they headed for the river nicknamed Big Muddy. The two longest rivers in the United States, the Missouri and the Mississippi, meet in the state of Missouri. These rivers made Missouri a gateway to the West—a place where pioneers began their westward travels.

Canoers on the Big Muddy

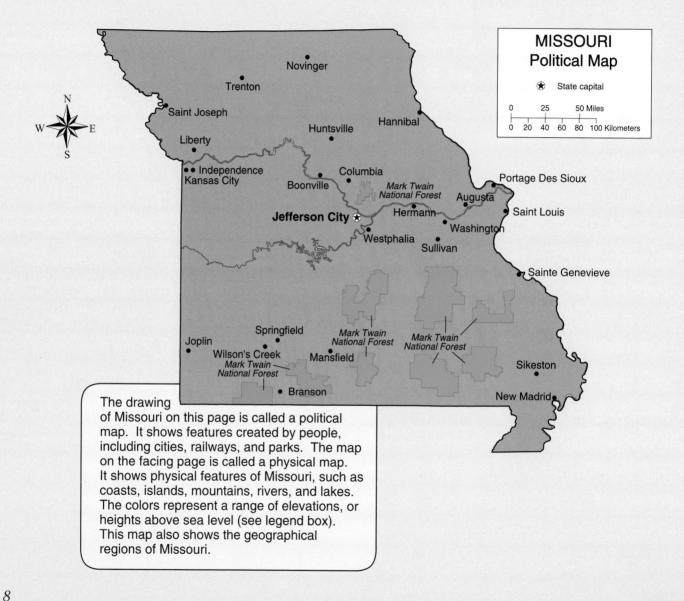

MISSOURI
Political Map

★ State capital

0   25   50 Miles

0   20   40   60   80   100 Kilometers

N
W   E
S

Novinger

Trenton

Saint Joseph

Liberty

Huntsville

Hannibal

Independence
Kansas City

Columbia

Boonville

Mark Twain
National Forest

Portage Des Sioux

Augusta

Saint Louis

Jefferson City ★

Hermann

Washington

Westphalia

Sullivan

Sainte Genevieve

Joplin

Springfield

Mark Twain
National Forest

Mark Twain
National Forest

Wilson's Creek

Mansfield

Sikeston

Mark Twain
National Forest

Branson

New Madrid

The drawing
of Missouri on this page is called a political
map. It shows features created by people,
including cities, railways, and parks. The map
on the facing page is called a physical map.
It shows physical features of Missouri, such as
coasts, islands, mountains, rivers, and lakes.
The colors represent a range of elevations, or
heights above sea level (see legend box).
This map also shows the geographical
regions of Missouri.

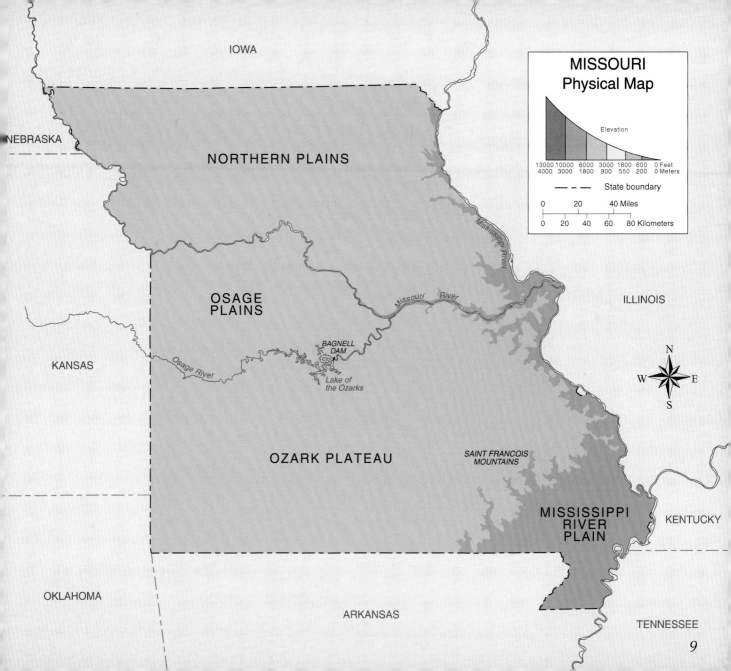

IOWA

NEBRASKA

KANSAS

OKLAHOMA

ARKANSAS

TENNESSEE

KENTUCKY

ILLINOIS

NORTHERN PLAINS

OSAGE
PLAINS

Osage River

BAGNELL
DAM

*Lake of
the Ozarks*

Missouri   River

Mississippi River

OZARK PLATEAU

SAINT FRANCOIS
MOUNTAINS

MISSISSIPPI
RIVER
PLAIN

MISSOURI
Physical Map

Elevation

13000 10000 6000 3000 1800 600   0 Feet
4000   3000   1800 900   550   200   0 Meters

State boundary

0   20   40 Miles

0   20   40   60   80 Kilometers

N
W   E
S

9

Wildflowers such as pale purple coneflowers color the prairies of western Missouri.

Missouri is surrounded by eight other states. To the east of the Mississippi River lie Illinois, Kentucky, and Tennessee. Other boundaries are formed by Arkansas, Oklahoma, Kansas, Nebraska, and Iowa. Only one other state, Tennessee, has as many neighbors.

Missouri has four geographic regions—the Northern Plains, the Osage Plains, the Ozark Plateau, and the Mississippi River Plain. During the **Ice Age** hundreds of thousands of years ago, **glaciers** moved into the Northern Plains. The huge, thick sheets of ice crept over the land, grinding up rocks and plants. In their path, the glaciers left rich soil and sand.

Streams wore through the dirt, carving hills in the Northern Plains. Forests grew in the eastern part of this region. Tall grasses sprouted over the western hills and the Osage Plains, the region in west central Missouri. Centuries of decaying grasses have made the flat **prairies** (grasslands) of the Osage Plains quite fertile.

The Ozark Plateau's rolling hills were formed millions of years ago.

Amazing rock formations can be found in Meramec Caverns and other caves.

Wooded hills and mountains blanket the Ozark Plateau, which covers most of southern Missouri. Millions of years ago, pressures deep underground pushed this region above the surrounding land, creating a **plateau.** A plateau is a large, relatively flat area that stands above the surrounding land. Rivers have since worn deep gorges into the plateau. The Saint Francois Mountains, the tallest in the state, stand in the southeastern part of the Ozark Plateau.

Mysterious sights hide beneath the surface of the Ozark Plateau. Water seeping down through the soil and bubbling up from underground springs has carved huge caves in the soft limestone. Icicle-like rock formations fascinate those who visit the caverns.

To the southeast, along the Mississippi River, sprawls the Mississippi River Plain. Called the Boot Heel because of its shape, this low flat plain was once a great **swamp,** or wetland. Farmers have drained the swamp to turn it into cropland.

Where the Mississippi River rolls past the Boot Heel, it is much wider and deeper than it is where it first enters the state. Some of the river's largest **tributaries**—the Missouri, Illinois, and Ohio Rivers—enter the Mississippi at points along Missouri's eastern border. These waters add to the Mississippi River, making it much bigger.

A Missouri farmer uses his tractor to bale hay grown in the Boot Heel.

Not all of Missouri's water makes its way to the Mississippi. Workers have dammed, or blocked, some rivers, especially on the Ozark Plateau. The backed-up waters have created the state's only large lakes. People enjoy swimming and fishing in the lakes, but they were built mainly to control floods and to supply **hydroelectric power.** Water flowing through the dams turns engines that create electricity.

Bagnell Dam on the Osage River backs up water for 130 miles to form the Lake of the Ozarks.

Missourians enjoy nature in their state's parks and forests.

Water also affects Missouri's weather. Farther down the Mississippi, moist air rises from the waters of the Gulf of Mexico, keeping most of Missouri humid and warm in the summer. Winter brings occasional snowfalls that range from 8 to 20 inches. But in Missouri's mild climate, snow usually melts in less than a week.

The warm air that comes from the Gulf of Mexico can become dangerous. Tornadoes form with little warning during spring and summer thunderstorms.

Twisters whirl across the state, leaving behind trails of flattened barns and uprooted trees.

Earthquakes also occasionally rock Missouri. In 1811 a major quake hit New Madrid, in the state's southeastern corner. Scientists predict that another major tremor will strike the state.

Overall, Missouri's weather is gentle enough to allow many plants and animals to thrive. One-third of the state is covered with stands of hardwood trees. Oak, hickory, and walnut trees provide food

This cave salamander makes its home in one of Missouri's caverns.

A beaver swims in one of Missouri's many streams.

for the white-tailed deer and wild turkeys that live in the lush forests.

Bobwhite quail feast on seeds along grassy borders of the woodlands. And beavers, nature's dam builders, create small ponds along Missouri's streams.

The first people to live in the Missouri area hunted mastodons.

THE HISTORY

Gateway to the West

Rivers have long been used as highways, and many people followed them to the land that would become Missouri. The first of these people arrived more than 10,000 years ago. These Native Americans, or Indians, lived in caves and ate the nuts, berries, and plants that they gathered. They hunted small and large animals, including mastodons—huge elephants that roamed North America after the last Ice Age.

Later, people who lived in the area learned to grow corn, beans, and squash. One tribe, the Missouri Indians, built villages on bluffs that overlooked the Missouri River.

Around A.D. 700 another group, the Mississippi Mound Builders, settled along the Mississippi River. These Indians became skilled farmers.

The thriving community of Cahokia was surrounded by outlying villages and fields. The Indians there built temple mounds for religious ceremonies.

Mound Builders raised enough crops to feed people living in large villages. Cahokia, near today's Saint Louis, was the largest Mississippian community.

By 1500 more than 30,000 Indians lived in Cahokia. Its location on the Mississippi River made it a trading center. Indians came to Cahokia to sell grizzly-bear teeth from the Rocky Mountains, sea-shells from the Gulf of Mexico, and copper from the region that later became Minnesota.

In the 1600s, the lives of both the Mississippian and Missouri Indians were destroyed. Although European explorers had not yet reached Missouri, their diseases had. Unaware that they were infect-ing others, traveling Indians who had been exposed to sick people from other tribes carried the diseases from village to village. By the late 1600s, many Mississippian and Missouri Indians had died, and the rest had fled their villages to escape illness.

Other tribes moved onto land abandoned by the Mississippian and Missouri Indians. From the east came the Kansa, Illinois, and Osage. The Osage built five villages on tributaries of the Missouri.

Marquette and Jolliet met Oto, Missouri, and Osage Indians as they explored the Missouri area.

Osage men shaved their eyebrows and heads, leaving only a small patch of hair on top of their heads.

Farmers and hunters, the Osage also raided neighboring tribes for food and slaves.

Meanwhile, European explorers had reached Missouri. Two Frenchmen, Jacques Marquette and Louis Jolliet, paddled canoes down the Mississippi River in 1673. In a diary of his travels, Marquette wrote that he was amazed at the huge, muddy river—the Missouri—that rushed into the Mississippi.

In 1682 René-Robert Cavelier, Sieur de La Salle, claimed for France the Mississippi and all the rivers that flowed into it. This vast piece of land stretched west from the Appalachians to the Rocky Mountains and south from Canada to the Gulf of Mexico. La Salle named the area Louisiana after the French king Louis XIV.

The first French settlers in the part of Louisiana that later became Missouri named their village Sainte Genevieve. Indians brought pelts to the riverside village to trade for blankets, mirrors, horses, guns, and liquor. By 1727 French miners were shipping lead from Sainte Genevieve all the way to New Orleans.

In 1764, 15-year-old René Auguste Chouteau traveled up the Mississippi River from New Orleans with his stepfather, Pierre Laclède. Just south of where the Missouri and Mississippi Rivers meet, the men built a fur-trading post called Laclède's Landing. They bought pelts from the Osage Indians. The fur trade thrived, and Laclède's Landing quickly grew into a busy French settlement—Saint Louis.

Indians exchanged furs for goods such as tobacco, buckshot, and glass beads at riverside trading posts.

For years the Chouteau family and the Osage trappers controlled the fur trade along the Missouri River. But life in the region began to change rapidly after 1803, when the United States bought all of Louisiana from France in a deal called the Louisiana Purchase.

Thomas Jefferson, the U.S. president, sent explorers Meriwether Lewis and William Clark to map the territory and to find a river route to the Pacific Ocean. Jefferson believed their discoveries would allow the United States to spread from the Atlantic to the Pacific coast. In 1804 the explorers left from Saint Louis and steered their boats up the Missouri River.

René Auguste Chouteau founded Saint Louis. His family built a fur-trading empire.

Missouri was the "Gateway to the West" because wagon trails that started there led settlers as far west as California.

The expedition lasted more than two years. Part of the route Lewis and Clark mapped later became the Oregon Trail. This was a wagon-train road that began in Missouri and ended on the West Coast.

The Lewis and Clark expedition encouraged a lot of people to move to Missouri. In 1812 the U.S. government established the Missouri Territory. As a territory, Missouri had to follow U.S. laws but had fewer rights than states did.

River trade expanded. In 1817 crowds gathered to watch a paddle-wheel steamboat dock in Saint

Louis's harbor for the first time. Able to carry large loads, steamers soon replaced the smaller boats in use. Pilots took the steamboats up the Missouri River to fur-trading posts as far away as Montana.

As more and more people traveled the rivers, Missouri's population grew. Missouri had attracted not only the French but also other pioneers. Many American Southerners moved into the area. With them they brought black slaves. Before long, nearly one out of every six people in the territory was a slave. Most were forced to work the land.

Daniel Boone *(above)*, the famous woodsman and pioneer, was among Missouri's early settlers. Steamboats *(left)* traveled the rivers carrying everything from settlers and tools to gamblers and circuses.

Pioneers built towns and farms throughout Missouri. The Indians in Missouri, however, were not happy about the change. Gradually, their hunting grounds shrank as white settlers plowed fields for corn and wheat. With less land, the Indians could no longer live as their ancestors had. At first, the tribes fought to defend their lands from settlers. But eventually, Indians in Missouri were forced to give up their territory and move farther west.

In the early 1800s, the territory had ample land, settlers, crops, and furs. Yet Missourians yearned for something more. In 1818 they asked the U.S. government to make their territory a state. But there was one problem.

Missourians who had come from the South wanted to keep their slaves. Many Americans, however, believed that slavery was wrong. Members of the U.S. Congress tried to keep the number of states that allowed slavery (slave states) equal to the number of states that did not allow slavery (free states).

If Missouri entered the Union as a slave state, there would be more slave states than free states. Missouri's request for statehood was delayed for two years, until Maine asked to enter the Union as a free state. To accept the two states, members of Congress struck a deal called the **Missouri Compromise.** On August 10, 1821, Missouri became the 24th state, a slave state.

Opposite page: Pioneers tried to bring everything that they would need for building new homes, such as this simple log cabin.

Mules pulled many of the covered wagons on the Oregon and Santa Fe trails.

The same year, a trader named William Becknell traced the Santa Fe Trail. This route followed an old trail made by Native Americans. It led 780 miles west from Independence, Missouri, to the city of Santa Fe in territory owned by Mexico.

In Santa Fe, traders from Missouri exchanged manufactured goods for silver and mules. This trade made some Missourians rich and gave the state one of its nicknames, the Mule State.

Merchants in Saint Louis grew rich selling supplies to the pioneers. Almost every day, steamboats packed with people, food, and tools left the city for Independence and posts farther up the Missouri River. Steamers chugged back down the river loaded with furs and sometimes with gold.

As more and more pioneers settled lands west of the Mississippi, U.S. citizens argued about whether to allow slavery in these new territories. The slave states in the South and the free states in the North

In 1849 Saint Louis's waterfront exploded in a mass of flames. A fire ravaged the port, destroying 23 steamboats and over $5 million worth of property.

could not settle their disagreements about slavery and other issues. In 1861 the Civil War broke out between the North and the South.

Most Missourians wanted their state to remain in the Union. But some of Missouri's leaders thought the state should join the Confederacy (a separate government formed by the Southern states).

The Dred Scott Decision

Dred Scott was a slave who lived in Missouri during the early 1800s. Scott's fight for freedom came to represent the country's fight over slavery.

As an adult, Scott moved around with his owner to states that did not allow slavery. When his owner died in Missouri, a slave state, Scott believed he should become a free man. He had, after all, lived in free states. Scott sued his master's widow for his freedom in 1846.

The trial for Scott's case was heard first by the Missouri Supreme Court in Saint Louis and then by the U.S. Supreme Court. Both courts agreed that Scott was still a slave.

In 1857 the U.S. Supreme Court ruled in the Dred Scott decision that black people were not U.S. citizens, and so they could not use the nation's court system. The Court also ruled that Congress could not ban slavery in U.S. territories.

After the Supreme Court made its decision, Scott was sold to a new owner, who freed the slave. But the court's ruling against Scott made many people angry. The Dred Scott decision gave Northerners and Southerners one more reason to begin the Civil War.

Missouri's governor, Claiborne Jackson, acted against the wishes of most Missourians when he commanded Missouri's troops to fight Union soldiers. The Union quickly gained control of northern Missouri.

Jackson and his supporters continued to operate out of southwestern Missouri, fighting a major battle at Wilson's Creek. After Jackson was defeated in 1862, **bushwhackers** and **jayhawkers** continued the violence. The opposing groups—bushwhackers supported the South and jayhawkers sided with the North—raided farms and towns and killed many people.

In 1865 the South surrendered, and the Civil War finally ended. But Missouri and the West were no longer the same. The war had ended slavery, and other changes also took place. Railroads were built across the country, and trains began moving goods once ferried on rivers or carried over wagon trails.

Union soldiers dug a channel through a swamp along the Mississippi River near New Madrid. This path allowed them to sneak a transport boat past a Confederate camp on one of the river's islands.

By the late 1800s, railroads linked towns and cities across the United States. Trains carried manufactured goods from Saint Louis or beef from Kansas City.

Steamboats, the former queens of the river, sat unused in their ports.

Though Missouri had lost some of its allure as an untamed land, its appeal was still strong. The state continued to grow, and its cities became important industrial and agricultural centers.

—— How Missouri "Framed" Jesse James ——

In this section of a mural painted by Thomas Hart Benton, Jesse James and his gang rob a train. Like several other bandits, James began robbing and killing as a bushwhacker during the Civil War. Before he was shot in 1882, James staged about 25 robberies.

Benton painted the mural on the walls of the state capitol in Jefferson City during the 1930s. Benton had captured the spirit of his native Missouri, but state lawmakers were outraged because he had not painted heroes and politicians. Instead, he illustrated the rascals and common people of the state—ruthless train robbers, dishonest fur traders, hardworking women, and escaping slaves.

During World War I (1914–1918), aging steamers went back to work. The steamers pushed barges loaded with food and manufactured goods down the Mississippi River to New Orleans. There, Missouri's products were loaded onto ships bound for Europe. River trade flourished again.

Missouri continued to develop industries throughout the 1900s. During World War II (1939–1945), the state's factories made supplies for the U.S. Army. Near the end of the war, Missourian Harry S. Truman became president of the United States.

In 1965 the Gateway Arch was built in Saint Louis as a reminder of Missouri's role as the Gateway to the West. From the top of the arch, viewers can see barges trailing the Mississippi. To the west lies

The Gateway Arch in Saint Louis is the tallest monument in the United States. It stands 630 feet high.

the land opened by hardworking traders, miners, and farmers.

In 1986 Missouri started a state lottery in order to raise money for environmental and education programs. During the 1990s, Missouri's economy remained strong. Farms were productive, and factories expanded in the cities. The state also focused on tourism, which has become a top-dollar industry for Missouri. Travelers are drawn to the Gateway to the West just as the pioneers were long ago.

Kansas City is Missouri's largest city.

PEOPLE & ECONOMY

Life in the Show Me State

I n 1899 a Missouri congressman, Willard Duncan Vandiver, claimed that fancy speeches did not impress him. He said, "I am from Missouri. You have got to show me." Since then, people have called Missouri the Show Me State.

About 5.6 million people live in the Show Me State. Seven out of every ten Missourians make their homes in cities. Kansas City, on Missouri's western border, is the state's largest city. Saint Louis, on the eastern side, ranks second in size.

Other major cities in Missouri include Saint Joseph, Columbia, Independence, Joplin, and Springfield. The state's capital, Jefferson City, was named for President Thomas Jefferson.

Most Missourians were born in the United States. About 84 percent have ancestors from European countries such as France, England, Germany, Czechoslovakia, Italy, and Ireland. People with African ancestors make up about 11 percent of the state's population. Smaller numbers of Missourians are Latino, Asian, or American Indian.

The people of Sainte Genevieve celebrate their French heritage each August during Jour de Fete.

Museums and historic sites throughout the state give visitors a peek into Missouri's past. Some of the area's oldest artworks are preserved at Washington State Park, where pictures of animals were carved into stone by Indians about 1,000 years ago.

At a historical park, students learn how to grind corn according to ancient Indian methods.

At Hannibal's annual Tom Sawyer Fence Painting Contest, neatness is not important.

The lives of Jesse James, George Washington Carver, Daniel Boone, and other people from the state's past are featured at historical exhibits. Missouri's history is also represented at the Harry S. Truman Library in Independence and on murals at the state capitol building in Jefferson City.

Dance, musicals, and plays entertain city audiences, while action-packed historical shows please crowds at vacation-area theaters. Missouri's musicians perform country, blues, jazz, and classical music.

No matter what the season, Missouri has a professional sports team in action. All winter, the Kansas City Blades and the Saint Louis Blues skate

for hockey honors. The Kansas City Wizards keep
major league soccer fans cheering.

Spring and summer bring out baseball fans wearing blue for the Kansas City Royals or red for the Saint Louis Cardinals. As fall approaches, the Kansas City Chiefs warm up to play football.

A number of highly skilled quarterbacks, including Warren Moon *(left),* Joe Montana, and Elvis Grbac, have played for the Kansas City Chiefs.

Outdoor Missouri offers fun for everyone. Real snow melts quickly in Missouri, but winter skiers enjoy gliding down slopes covered with machine-made snow. Canoeing and river rafting are popular summer activities. And each year millions of vacationers visit the state's parks and lakes.

Missouri's recreational opportunities make living and working in the state attractive to many people. Almost two-thirds of the Missourians who work

Fishing is a popular activity on Missouri's lakes and rivers.

At a factory in Saint Louis, workers assemble vans.

have service jobs. Workers in service jobs help other people or businesses. These workers include teachers, doctors, sales people, and car mechanics.

Many service workers earn their living helping others enjoy their stay in Missouri. Some operate resorts on lakes and rivers. Food servers, hotel clerks, and entertainers also help make tourism one of Missouri's most important businesses.

Some government workers also help vacationers enjoy their stays in Missouri. Rangers welcome campers at the state and national parks. Other government workers work in hospitals and on military bases. About 13 percent of working Missourians are employed by the government.

Another 13 percent of Missouri's workers hold jobs in factories. Most of these people have jobs in the Saint Louis and Kansas City areas.

A river barge carries products from Missouri to ports elsewhere in the United States.

Some factory workers in Missouri tend machines that produce chemicals for farms and industries. Other factory workers are skilled mechanics who build cars, truck bodies, railroad cars, barges, or airplanes.

Missouri's river highways and the state's history as a trading center led to another major industry—transportation. Saint Louis and Kansas City are hubs for truck, railroad, airline, and river barge traffic. Many products are shipped by barge from Saint Louis to other U.S. ports. And the grain loaded in Saint Louis or Kansas City may end up almost anywhere in the world.

Kansas City has been a meat-packing and flour-milling town ever since workers built a railroad bridge across the Missouri River in 1869. From the country's western plains, trains transport cattle and wheat across the bridge to Kansas City.

Meat-processing plants in Missouri butcher cows and pigs. Kansas City's mills rank second in the nation for grinding wheat into flour.

Missouri's pigs eat corn and other grains that grow in the state.

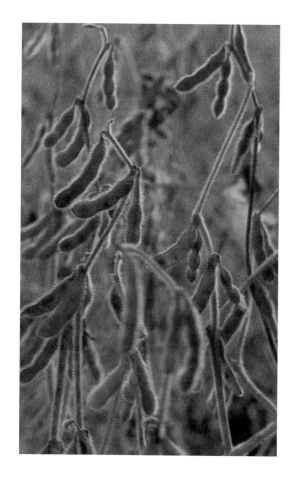

Soybeans grow well on Missouri's prairie. They are the state's most important crop.

Farmers in the state grow many crops. On the prairies and rolling hills in northern and central Missouri, farmers plant soybeans and corn. The Mississippi River Plain provides rich soil for growing cotton and rice. The hilly lands of the Ozark Plateau are difficult to farm, but the area is good for grazing beef and dairy cattle and for growing wheat.

A few of Missouri's workers are keeping some old traditions alive. Lead, which was mined by Missouri's first French settlers, is still found in large quantities in the state's southern counties.

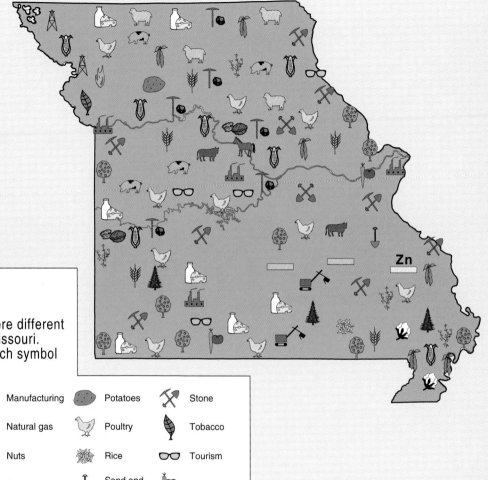

MISSOURI
Economic Map

The symbols on this map show where different economic activities take place in Missouri. The legend below explains what each symbol stands for.

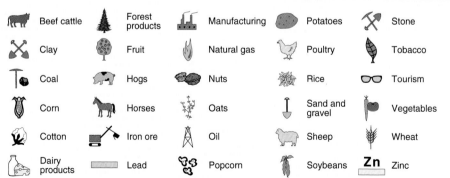

Symbol	Name	Symbol	Name	Symbol	Name	Symbol	Name	Symbol	Name
	Beef cattle		Forest products		Manufacturing		Potatoes		Stone
	Clay		Fruit		Natural gas		Poultry		Tobacco
	Coal		Hogs		Nuts		Rice		Tourism
	Corn		Horses		Oats		Sand and gravel		Vegetables
	Cotton		Iron ore		Oil		Sheep		Wheat
	Dairy products		Lead		Popcorn		Soybeans	Zn	Zinc

Missourians celebrate their German heritage with polka music at Hermann's Maifest.

Missouri produces more lead than any other state. Workers also mine coal and iron from the Ozark hills.

German settlers came to the Hermann area in central Missouri because it reminded them of the grape-growing valleys of Germany. Hermann's wine makers still crush grapes to make wine. Another German tradition—beer making—is followed at the Anheuser-Busch brewery in Saint Louis. And, as a clear reminder of pioneer days, Missouri is still the nation's top breeder of mules.

To produce electricity, power plants in Missouri burn coal that is strip-mined in the state.

THE ENVIRONMENT

Protecting Missouri's Wildlife

Wild turkey

For the Native Americans who once lived in the area, Missouri was a land of plenty. Huge herds of bison (buffalo) grazed on the grassy plains. Deer and wild turkeys roamed the forests. And the rivers were swimming with catfish, beavers, and otters. Each spring and fall, migrating ducks and geese filled the skies.

When the French trappers arrived, life became more difficult for Missouri's wildlife. The trappers killed many animals for their furs. Then settlers began clearing woodlands and prairies to make room for crops. Later, hunters killed birds by the thousands and shipped them to restaurants on the East Coast, where menus featured wild quail and duck.

A Missouri plain *(left)* in bloom. Many plains were cleared so settlers could plant crops. Bison *(below)*, or buffalo, were hunted for their coats and their meat.

By the late 1920s, hunters had killed all the buffalo, deer, and wild turkeys in the state. Then came the Great Depression. Many people lost their jobs. They hunted wild animals to feed their families. Within 10 years, nearly all of Missouri's game animals were gone.

The disappearance of animals troubled many Missourians. In 1937 Missouri became the first state to start a department of conservation. This new government office planned to base its hunting and fishing rules on research about animals.

At the Mingo National Wildlife Refuge, bald cypress trees shed their leaves for autumn. These and other government-owned lands provide havens for Missouri's wild animals.

Missouri's streams are home to river otters.

Since the Department of Conservation was formed, scientists have studied the types of food and shelter needed by different plants and animals. Researchers also find out how animals raise their young. The department uses this information to help plant and animal populations survive and grow.

Many organizations have helped Missouri's Department of Conservation protect the habitats of various animals. By buying and preserving areas in the state that provide natural habitats, these groups make certain that wild animals will be able to find the food and shelter they need.

White-tailed deer inhabit forests in the Ozarks.

An early success came at the end of the 1930s. The state government brought a few deer back into the state, then banned deer hunting. In the following years, the deer raised many fawns. Slowly, the number of these animals began to rise. Once the deer population became large enough, limited hunting was allowed.

Wildlife scientists have brought back other animals that had disappeared from the state. Not long ago, all the state's wild turkeys, bald eagles, Canada geese, trumpeter swans, ruffed grouse, and river otters were gone. Because of successful wildlife programs, all of these animals are again thriving and raising young in Missouri.

Although some animals can be hunted without harming their populations, others, such as the prairie chicken, may never be hunted again. Most of this bird's habitat—the prairie—has been planted with crops. Missouri will probably never again have enough natural grassland to support a large number of prairie chickens.

Prairie chickens attract mates by dancing.

Laws protect animal populations in Missouri by controlling the number of animals that hunters are allowed to kill each year.

All Missourians contribute to the state's wildlife programs. In 1976 the people of the state voted to raise taxes to help fund the Department of Conservation. In 1998, funding was provided to restore the natural habitats of Missouri's endangered species. A special emphasis was placed on prairie habitat restoration. Missourians are proud of their many fish and wildlife refuges which preserve and restore the natural habitats of birds, mammals, reptiles, and amphibians.

Huge herds of buffalo may never again thunder across Missouri's plains. But nature lovers can watch for the flight of a bald eagle, the leap of a deer, and the splash of a beaver's tail. By working together, Missourians have maintained a home for wildlife in their state.

ALL ABOUT MISSOURI

Fun Facts

Missouri takes its name from the Missouri River. The name may mean "muddy water" or "people of the large canoes" in the language of the Missouri Indians.

Lake of the Ozarks in central Missouri has a winding shoreline that runs 1,375 miles. That's longer than the Pacific Coast of California!

The first people to taste hot dogs and ice cream cones were visitors at the Saint Louis World's Fair in 1904.

Saint Louis World's Fair, 1904

Early traders floated furs down Missouri's rivers in crafts called bull boats. The boats were made of willow saplings covered with buffalo hides. Only male, or bull, skins were used because female hides leaked too easily.

The first person to parachute from an airplane was Captain Albert Berry in 1912. He jumped from 1,500 feet and landed at Jefferson Barracks in Saint Louis, Missouri, using a modified hot air balloon.

Washington, Missouri, produces 6 million corncob pipes every year, making it the world's largest manufacturer of the unique pipes.

In 1873 Susan Elizabeth Blow taught the first kindergarten class when the Saint Louis Board of Education opened public schools to students of such a young age.

Jesse James

America's first daylight bank robbery occurred on February 13, 1866, in Liberty, Missouri. Bandits stole more than $60,000 from the Clay County Savings Bank and Loan Association. The case was never solved, but many people believe the famous criminal Jesse James staged the robbery.

STATE SONG

The melody for Missouri's state song was written in 1914, and the words were added two years later. The song was a popular hit of the time and was adopted as Missouri's official state song in 1949. "Missouri Waltz" was also President Harry S. Truman's theme song.

MISSOURI WALTZ

Music by John Valentine Eppel, as arranged by Frederic Knight Logan
Lyrics by James Royce Shannon

Hush-a-bye, ma ba-by, slum-ber time is com-in' soon; Rest yo' head up-on my breast while Mom-my hums a tune; The sand-man is call-in' where shad-ows are fall-in' While the soft breez-es sigh as in days long gone by. Way down in Mis-sou-ri where I heard this mel-o-dy, When I was a lit-tle child on my Mom-my's knee; The old folks were hum-in' Their ban-jos were strum-min' So sweet and low

You can hear "Missouri Waltz" by visiting this website:
<http://www.50states.com/songs/mo.htm>

A MISSOURI RECIPE

Toasted ravioli is a popular appetizer in many
Saint Louis restaurants. According to local legend,
the dish was first made when a cook accidentally
dropped a ravioli into a pan of hot oil. At certain times of the year, 400,000 ravioli
are produced every day in Saint Louis—about one for every person in the city.

SAINT LOUIS TOASTED RAVIOLI

2 tablespoons whole milk
1 egg
¾ cup Italian seasoned bread crumbs
½ teaspoon salt
½ (25 ounce) package frozen meat or cheese ravioli, thawed
3 cups vegetable oil
1 tablespoon grated Parmesan cheese
1 jar marinara sauce

1. Combine milk and egg in small bowl.
2. Place bread crumbs and salt in shallow bowl.
3. Dip thawed ravioli in milk mixture, then coat with bread crumbs.
4. In saucepan, heat sauce over medium heat until bubbling. Reduce heat, simmer.
5. Pour oil, about 2 inches deep, into large heavy pan. Heat oil over medium heat until
   small amount of breading dropped into pan sizzles and turns brown.
6. Have an adult help you carefully drop ravioli, two or three at a time, into the pan. Fry one
   minute on each side or until golden. Remove from pan with slotted spoon, put on paper
   towels to dry and cool slightly.
7. Sprinkle ravioli with Parmesan cheese and serve immediately with hot marinara sauce.

HISTORICAL TIMELINE

13,000 B.C. Early Indians hunt mastodons in the area later called Missouri.

A.D. 700 Indians settle in villages along the Mississippi River.

1500 More than 30,000 Indians live in Cahokia.

1673 Marquette and Jolliet explore the Mississippi River.

1682 La Salle claims the Mississippi Valley, including Missouri, for France. He names the area Louisiana.

1764 Chouteau and Laclède build a fur-trading outpost near what later became Saint Louis.

1803 The United States buys a large portion of land from France, including what later became Missouri, in a deal called the Louisiana Purchase.

1811 A major earthquake hits New Madrid, in the state's southeast corner.

1812 The U.S. Congress makes Missouri a territory.

1815 Indian attacks on Missouri settlements end after Indians and U.S. government officials sign a peace treaty at Portage Des Sioux.

1821 Missouri becomes the 24th state.

1846 Dred Scott sues his master's widow for his freedom.

1861 The Civil War (1861–1865) begins and splits the state.

1882 Outlaw Jesse James dies in Saint Joseph.

1904 The World's Fair in Saint Louis celebrates the 100th anniversary of the Louisiana Purchase.

1931 Bagnell Dam on the Osage River is completed, forming the Lake of the Ozarks.

1945 Missourian Harry S. Truman becomes president of the United States.

1965 The Gateway Arch is built in Saint Louis.

1986 The state's government begins to operate a statewide lottery.

1993 Severe floods strike Missouri, damaging billions of dollars worth of property and crops.

1998 Saint Louis Cardinal Mark McGwire sets a baseball record with 70 home runs in a single season.

OUTSTANDING MISSOURIANS

Ed Asner

Ed Asner (born 1929) worked on his first newspaper in high school in Kansas City, Missouri. The actor became known to television viewers as newsman Lou Grant on both *The Mary Tyler Moore Show* and *Lou Grant.*

Josephine Baker (1906–1975), a dancer and singer, was born in Saint Louis. She found fame in Paris, France, with her racy performances. During World War II in France, she worked to defeat the Germans, and during the 1950s and 1960s in the United States, she worked to gain equal rights for African Americans.

Josephine Baker

Thomas Hart Benton (1782–1858) represented Missouri in the U.S. Senate for 30 years, from 1821 until 1851. He was strongly in favor of expanding the United States west across North America.

Thomas Hart Benton (1889–1975) was named for his great-uncle, the politician. His murals are known for their strong lines and bright colors as well as the Midwest and Southern scenes they portray.

Yogi Berra

Lawrence "Yogi" Berra (born 1925), a native of Saint Louis, was a catcher for the Yankees from 1946 to 1963. He holds the record for playing in the most (14) World Series. In 1965 Berra began coaching for the New York Mets, and in 1972 he became manager of that team. Berra is also known for his love of comic books.

Chuck Berry (born 1926) is a guitarist and singer who helped change the sound of popular American music. Berry started out playing blues music in Saint Louis, his hometown. His real success came when he began playing rock and roll in the late 1950s. Berry's hits include "Sweet Little Sixteen," and "Johnny B. Goode."

Chuck Berry

George Caleb Bingham (1811–1879) was a painter who lived in Missouri from the time he was eight years old. He made his living painting portraits, but he is remembered for his scenes of frontier life.

Adolphus Busch (1839–1913) emigrated from Germany to Saint Louis and married the daughter of a beer brewer named Anheuser. Busch became president of Anheuser's company and renamed it Anheuser-Busch. Busch was among the first to pasteurize beer and make it possible to ship beer long distances without refrigeration.

George Caleb Bingham

George Washington Carver (1864–1943) was born near Diamond, Missouri. Carver was interested in plants and became a leading agricultural scientist. He is best known for products that he created from peanuts, including meal, ink, linoleum, and plastics.

Adolphus Busch

Walt Disney (1901–1966) grew up in Marceline and in Kansas City, Missouri. Disney pioneered the use of animation in movies. His cartoon characters, such as Mickey Mouse, are known around the world. Disney also built the theme parks Disneyland and Disney World.

Edwin Powell Hubble (1889–1953), born in Marshfield, Missouri, was an astronomer who changed the way we look at the universe. Hubble proved that many other galaxies lie far outside our Milky Way. The first space telescope, which the United States launched in 1990, is named for Hubble.

Walt Disney

Langston Hughes (1902–1967), a native of Joplin, Missouri, used street language and the musical rhythms of the blues to write about the lives of black people. His poetry, novels, and plays made him one of the greatest American writers of the 20th century. His works include *Weary Blues* and *Not Without Laughter*.

Langston Hughes

Scott Joplin

J.C. Penney

Vincent Price

Ginger Rogers

Frank James (1843–1915) and **Jesse James** (1847–1882) were two famous outlaws of the American West. Between 1866 and 1882, the brothers and their gang of bandits robbed trains, stagecoaches, banks, stores, and individual people all over the western United States. The brothers were born in Centerville, Missouri.

Scott Joplin (1868–1917) was a musician who settled in Sedalia, Missouri, in 1896. There he developed his own style of jazz piano, called ragtime. His best-known tunes include "Maple Leaf Rag" and "The Entertainer."

James Cash Penney (1875–1971), a native of Hamilton, Missouri, founded the J. C. Penney department-store chain. In 1902 he opened his first general store, called the Golden Rule. At the time of Penney's death in 1971, his company had 1,640 stores and sales had topped $4.8 billion.

Vincent Price (1911–1993) was born in Saint Louis. The actor is best known for his chilling roles as villains in horror movies. He starred in over 100 films over seven decades. His movies include *House of Usher, The Masque of the Red Death*, and *Edward Scissorhands*.

Ginger Rogers (1911–1995), originally known as Virginia Katherine McMath, was an actress and dancer who was born in Independence, Missouri. She became famous for the musical films she starred in with dance partner Fred Astaire. Rogers won an Academy Award in 1940 for her role in *Kitty Foyle*.

Michael Spinks (born 1956) is a champion boxer who grew up in Saint Louis. Spinks gained fans all across the United States when he and his brother Leon each won gold medals in boxing at the 1976 Olympic Games.

Charles "Casey" Stengel (1890-1975), a native of Kansas City, Missouri, was one of baseball's most beloved personalities. An outfielder and later a manager, he was always a comedian on the field. Stengel managed the New York Yankees for 12 years and won 10 pennants, including five straight World Series.

Harry S. Truman (1884–1972) grew up in Independence, Missouri. In 1944 President Franklin Roosevelt chose Truman to run for the office of vice-president of the United States. Just 83 days after being sworn into office, Roosevelt died and Truman became president. He served as president from 1945 to 1953.

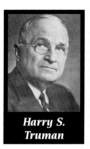

Harry S. Truman

Kathleen Turner (born 1954) grew up in Springfield, Missouri. An actress, Turner has starred in many movies, including *Romancing the Stone*, *The Accidental Tourist*, and *War of the Roses*.

Kathleen Turner

Mark Twain (1835–1910) is the pen name used by author Samuel Clemens, who grew up in Hannibal, Missouri. Twain developed an American style of writing using the everyday speech he had heard in Hannibal. Two of his best-known books are *The Adventures of Tom Sawyer* and *The Adventures of Huckleberry Finn*.

Mark Twain

Laura Ingalls Wilder (1867–1957) settled in Mansfield, Missouri, in 1894. There, at the age of 60, she began to write a children's series called the "Little House" books. These stories describe Wilder's childhood on the plains of the Midwest.

Roy Wilkins (1901–1981) was born in Saint Louis. From 1955 to 1977 he served as executive secretary for the National Association for the Advancement of Colored People (NAACP). He was known for his thoughtful leadership and for using the court system to protect the rights of black people.

Roy Wilkins

FACTS-AT-A-GLANCE

Nickname: Show Me State

Song: "Missouri Waltz"

Motto: *Salus populi suprema lex esto*
(The welfare of the people shall be
supreme law)

Flower: hawthorn

Tree: flowering dogwood

Bird: bluebird

Fish: channel catfish

Insect: honeybee

Fossil: crinoid

Date and ranking of statehood:
August 10, 1821, the 24th state

Capital: Jefferson City

Area: 68,898 square miles

Rank in area, nationwide: 18th

Average January temperature: 30° F

Average July temperature: 78° F

Adopted in 1913, Missouri's state flag has
stripes of red, white, and blue to show the
state's loyalty to the United States. The ring
of stars represents Missouri's entry into the
Union as the 24th state. The flag also features
Missouri's state seal.

POPULATION GROWTH

Millions

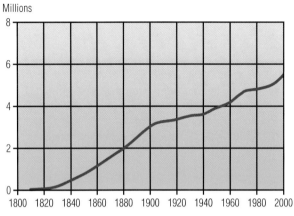

This chart shows how Missouri's population has grown from 1810 to 2000.

The bears on Missouri's official state seal represent the state's strength and the bravery of its citizens. The bears hold a shield that shows symbols of Missouri.

Population: 5,595,211 (2000 census)

Rank in population, nationwide: 17th

Major cities and populations: (2000 census) Kansas City (441,545), Saint Louis (348,189), Springfield (151,580), Independence (113,288), Columbia (84,531), Saint Joseph (73,990)

U.S. senators: 2

U.S. representatives: 9

Electoral votes: 11

Natural resources: clay, coal, fertile soil, forests, iron ore, lead, stone, water, zinc

Agricultural products: beef cattle, chickens, corn, cotton, dairy cattle, eggs, hay, horses, mules, pigs, popcorn, rice, sheep, soybeans, turkeys, wheat

Manufactured goods: airplanes, automobiles, barges, chemicals, machinery, paper and printed materials, railroad cars, steel, truck and bus bodies

WHERE MISSOURIANS WORK

Services—64 percent (services includes jobs in trade; community, social, and personal services; finance, insurance, and real estate; transportation, communication, and utilities)

Manufacturing—13 percent

Government—13 percent

Construction—6 percent

Agriculture and fishing—4 percent

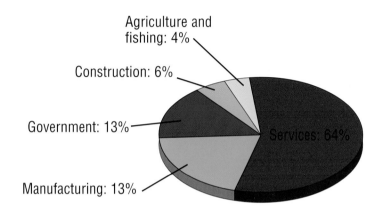

Agriculture and fishing: 4%

Construction: 6%

Government: 13%

Manufacturing: 13%

Services: 64%

GROSS STATE PRODUCT

Services—60 percent

Manufacturing—21 percent

Government—11 percent

Construction—5 percent

Agriculture and fishing—3 percent

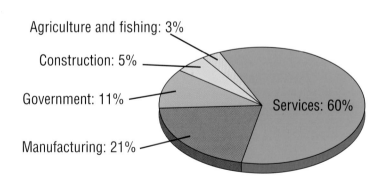

Agriculture and fishing: 3%

Construction: 5%

Government: 11%

Manufacturing: 21%

Services: 60%

STATE WILDLIFE

Mammals: beaver, black bear, flying squirrel, fox, masked shrew, mountain lion, muskrat, opossum, rabbit, raccoon, skunk, squirrel, white-tailed deer

Birds: bluebird, blue jay, bobwhite quail, cardinal, great blue heron, mockingbird, painted bunting, prairie falcon, purple finch, roadrunner, ruby-throated hummingbird, woodpecker

Amphibians and reptiles: alligator, king snake, western slender glass lizard, snapping turtle, wood frog

Fish: bass, bluegill, channel catfish, crappie, jack salmon, longear sunfish, muskellunge, small mouth bass

Trees: bald cypress, cottonwood, flowering dogwood, maple, northern red oak, shortleaf pine, slippery elm, sweet gum, white ash

Wild plants: anemones, asters, dogwood, dwarf larkspur, eastern witch hazel, fragrant sumac, ginseng, goldenrod, milkweed, mint, roses, verbina, violet, water milfoil, white snakeroot

Dogwood blossoms

PLACES TO VISIT

Branson
Located in the southwestern Missouri Ozarks, this town is home to theme parks and more than 40 theaters which offer live musical performances throughout the year. Branson is a center for country music lovers from all over the country.

Children's Peace Pavilion, Independence
At this interactive children's museum, young people can explore exhibits about different concepts of peace.

Gateway Arch, Saint Louis
Visitors can ride to the top of the 630-foot arch in small trains. The arch symbolizes Missouri's part in settling the west.

Harry S. Truman Library, Independence
Located in the former U.S. president's hometown, this library houses over 3 million documents and other artifacts from Truman's presidency.

Mark Twain Cave, near Hannibal
Mark Twain explored this cave located near his home as a boy. Later, he wrote about it in one of his books—it's the cave where Tom and Becky get lost in *The Adventures of Tom Sawyer*.

Mark Twain Home and Museum, Hannibal
The boyhood home of the author has been restored. A museum next door exhibits many objects related to Mark Twain's life.

Meramec Caverns, near Sullivan
The largest cave in Missouri that's open to visitors is over 400 million years old. Jesse James, the legendary outlaw, once used this cave as his hideout.

Missouri Botanical Garden, Saint Louis
This large garden offers educational programs, mazes, and horticultural exhibits. Each section of the garden has a special theme.

Painted Rock Conservation Area, near Westphalia
Hikers can explore steep trails overlooking the Osage River and its colorful rock formations.

Pony Express Musuem, Saint Joseph
These former stables have been transformed into a museum that tells about the famous Pony Express. Horses and riders of the Pony Express carried mail from Saint Joseph to Sacramento, California, from April 1860 to October 1861.

Silver Dollar City, near Branson
This theme park combines amusement park rides with 1890s Ozark culture. Between roller coaster rides, visitors can learn about old-fashioned Missouri crafts and other historical activities.

Visitors tour Mark Twain Cave.

ANNUAL EVENTS

Lake Lights Festival, Lake of the Ozarks—*January*

Old Time Fiddler's Contest, Boonville—*January*

World Fest, Branson—*April*

Strawberry Festival, Augusta—*May*

Coal Miner Days, Novinger—*May*

Huntsville Horse Show, Huntsville—*June*

Ragtime Festival, Saint Louis—*June*

Tom Sawyer Fence Painting Contest, Hannibal—*July*

Boot Heel Rodeo, Sikeston—*August*

Jour de Fete, Sainte Genevieve—*August*

Wilder Festival, Mansfield—*September*

Octoberfest, Hermann—*October*

Missouri Day Festival, Trenton—*October*

LEARN MORE ABOUT MISSOURI

BOOKS

General

Hintz, Martin. *Missouri*. Danbury, CT: Children's Press, 1999.

McCandless, Perry and William E. Foley. *Missouri Then and Now*. Columbia, MO: University of Missouri Press, 1992. For older readers.

Thompson, Kathleen. *Missouri*. Orlando, FL: Raintree/Steck-Vaughn, 1996.

Special Interest

Bowen, Andy Russell. *The Back of Beyond*. Minneapolis: Carolrhoda Books, Inc., 1997. Explorers Meriwether Lewis and William Clark started their famous trek across the American West in Saint Louis. This book follows them from Missouri to the Pacific Ocean.

Doherty, Craig A. *The Gateway Arch*. Woodbridge, CT: Blackbirch Marketing, 1995. Black-and-white and full-color photographs and text describe the construction of the arch.

Wilder, Laura Ingalls. *On the Way Home*. New York: HarperTrophy, 1994. The diary of the famous author of the *Little House* books covers her family's journey from South Dakota to their new home in Mansfield, Missouri.

Fiction

Horvath, Polly. *The Happy Yellow Car.* New York: Farrar, Straus & Giroux, 1994. This humorous book set in the Missouri Ozarks is about Betty Grunt, a 12-year-old who loses her college fund when her father buys a yellow car to be used only for Sunday drives.

Garrity, Jennifer Johnson. *The Bushwhacker: A Civil War Adventure.* Atlanta, GA: Peachtree Publishers, 1999. Set during the Civil War, this illustrated novel tells the story of two siblings in Missouri. After their family is terrorized by Confederate supporters known as bushwhackers, Jacob and Eliza are forced to leave home.

Nixon, Joan Lowery. *Keeping Secrets.* New York: Laurel Leaf Books, 1996. Set in Missouri during the Civil War, this adventure novel follows 11-year-old Peg Kelly as she unknowingly becomes involved with a Union spy.

Twain, Mark. *The Adventures of Huckleberry Finn.* New York: Aladdin Paperbacks, 1999. Readers have long enjoyed following Huck Finn on his adventures on the Mississippi River. This version of the American classic includes recently discovered and previously unpublished material.

WEBSITES

Missouri State Government Home Page
<http://www.state.mo.us/>
Missouri's official website provides links to state organizations, departments, and services as well as an information and game page for kids.

Official Missouri Division of Tourism Homepage
<http://www.missouritourism.org>
This official tourism site includes places to stay, things to do, and annual events in the Show Me State.

The Digital Missourian
<http://digmo.org/>
Read about the latest news in Missouri in this online newspaper based in Columbia.

Kansas City Museum
<http://www.kcmuseum.com>
The official site for the Kansas City Museum and Science City at Union Station provides information about activities at each attraction.

The Nature Page
<http://www.conservation.state.mo.us/nathis>
The Missouri Department of Conservation's Nature Page shows and describes the seven hundred species of fish and wildlife that live in the state.

PRONUNCIATION GUIDE

Anheuser-Busch (AN-hy-sur BUSH)

Chouteau, René Auguste (shoo-TOH, reh-NAY oh GOOST)

Jolliet, Louis (JOH-lee-eht, LOO-his)

Laclède, Pierre (lah-KLEHD, pee-AIR)

La Salle, René-Robert Cavelier, Sieur de (luh SAL, ruh-NAY-roh-BEHR
  ka-vuhl-YAY, SYER duh)

Marquette, Jacques (mahr-KEHT, zhahk)

New Orleans (noo OR-lee-uhns)

Osage (oh-SAYJ)

Ozark Plateau (OH-zahrk pla-TOH)

Sainte Genevieve (saynt JEHN-uh-veev)

Saint Francois (saynt FRAN-suhs)

Rapids in the Big
Springs Area

GLOSSARY

bushwhacker: someone who attacks others from a position of hiding. During the Civil War, bushwhackers were Confederate soliders who worked independently, raiding and destroying the property of people who supported the Union.

glacier: a large body of ice and snow that moves slowly over land

hydroelectric power: the electricity produced by using waterpower; also called hydropower

ice age: a period when ice sheets cover large regions of the earth. The term *Ice Age* usually refers to the most recent one, called the Pleistocene, which began almost 2 million years ago and ended about 10,000 years ago.

jayhawker: a member of a pro-Union group that staged raids in Missouri before and during the Civil War

Missouri Compromise: an agreement made by the U.S. Congress in 1820 to admit Missouri into the Union as a slave state and Maine as a free state

plateau: a large, relatively flat area that stands above the surrounding land

prairie: a large area of level or gently rolling grassy land with few trees

swamp: a wetland permanently soaked with water. Woody plants (trees and shrubs) are the main form of vegetation.

tributary: a river or stream that feeds, or flows into, a larger river

INDEX

PHOTO ACKNOWLEDGMENTS

© William A. Bake/Corbis, cover (left); © Richard Cummins/Corbis, cover (right); Digital Cartographics, pp. 1, 8, 9, 49; © David Muench/Corbis, p. 2-3; © Buddy Mays/Corbis, p. 3; Karlene V. Schwartz, p. 4 (detail), 7(detail), 13, 19(detail), 39(detail), 52(detail), 73; © Craig Aurness/Corbis, p. 6; Ron Spomer/Visuals Unlimited, p.7; Jim Rathert/ Missouri Department of Conservation, pp. 10, 11, 15, 44, 52, 53 (top), 56, 57, 58 (top); Permission granted by the Missouri Division of Tourism, pp. 12, 14, 30, 40, 42, 46, 50, 53 (bottom right); Richard Thom/Visuals Unlimited, pp. 16, 51; © Len Rue, Jr. 135,111, p. 17; Mark Hallett, p. 18; Cahokia Mounds State Historical Site, pp. 20, 41; Missouri Historical Society, pp. 22 (left-neg. #110a), 22 (top- J.N. Marchand, neg. #4a), 25 (neg. C-6a), 31, 60 (neg#862), 62; Thomas Gilcrease Institute of American History and Art, Tulsa, Oklahoma, p. 24; Laura Westland, p. 26; Saint Louis Mercantile Library Association, pp. 27 (bottom), 34; Ohio Historical Society, p. 27 (right); Kent & Donna Dannen, pp. 28, 54, 58 (bottom), 75; Library of Congress, p. 32, 66 (second from top), 69 (top); New Madrid Historical Museum, p. 33; Missouri Department of Natural Resources, p. 35; University of Louisville, Kentucky, Ford Album Collection, p. 36 (neg. # 77.1.314); © James Rowan, p. 37; © Joseph Sohm; ChromoSohm Inc./Corbis, p. 38; © ALLSPORT USA/Stephen Dunn, p. 43; Chrysler Corporation, p. 45; Missouri Farm Bureau, pp. 47, 48; Len Rue, Jr./Visuals Unlimited, p. 55; Archive Photos, p. 61; Tim Seeley, p. 63; State Historical Society of Missouri, p. 67 (top); National Baseball Hall of Fame & Museum Inc., p. 66 (second from bottom); Hollywood Book and Poster Company, pp. 66 (top, and bottom), 67 (second from bottom), 69 (second from top); Anheuser-Busch Corporation Archives, p. 67 (second from top); Dodd, Mead, and Company Inc., p. 67 (bottom); New York Public Library, Astor, Lenox & Tilden Foundations, p. 68 (top); J. C. Penney Company Inc., p. 68 (second from top); Photofest, p. 68 (second from bottom); © Superstock, p. 68 (bottom); Hannibal Convention & Visitors Bureau, p. 69 (second from bottom); Independent Picture Service, p. 69 (bottom); Jean Matheny, p. 70; Maryland Cartographics, pp. 72; © Susan Day/Daybreak Imagery, p. 80.